Something To Be Proud Of

EILEEN DISTASIO-CLARK

With Great Love and Appreciation to Those Who Have and Do Bless My Life.

My Family:

Joseph DeStasio Sr. & Miriam Lucille Baragone DeStasio, My Late Parents.

Andrea Jean DeStasio McIntosh, My Older Sister and Their Families.

Joseph DeStasio Jr., My Younger and Only Brother and Their Families.

Donna Marie DeStasio Wagner, My Younger Sister and Their Families.

My Children:

Eileen, Rebekah, Rachel, S. Michael,

Jennifer, Sharon, Tara, Stephanie,

Apryll, Mikaelah, & M. Trevor

and THEIR Families!!

ACKNOWLEDGEMENTS

First and foremost, I express, deeply, my sincere gratitude to our Heavenly Father for blessing me with the gift and talent of writing! I know I could not do what I do without His assistance.

I also want to acknowledge and express gratitude to the members of my birth family—Joseph Sr., Miriam, Andrea, Joseph Junior, and Donna. All the experiences of my childhood years, experiences that taught me so very much and enabled me to reveal my true self to myself, came about through my experiences and relationships with them.

And, of course, it goes without saying, but I will say it anyway: I also want to acknowledge and note my gratitude to my children, Eileen, Rebekah, Rachel, S. Michael, Jennifer, Sharon, Tara, Stephanie, Apryll, Mikaelah, and M. Trevor, and their families! Through multiple things they said to me, over multiple years, I finally came to the realization that

Heavenly Father gave me the gift of writing and opened the doors to these experiences because He knew that by sharing them with others, others could feel His love too.

And He definitely wants us all to know that He, Heavenly Father, Heavenly Mother, and Jehovah truly do loves us!!!

INTRODUCTION

There are sixteen books in this series, which I refer to as *"The Ellie Series."* All of the characters in these stories portray real people from my life. The main characters depict the members of my family: Daddy is my daddy; Mommy is my mommy; Jeannie is my older sister; Junior is my brother; Maria is my younger sister, and Ellie is me. Now, those are not our actual first names, but they do reference us.

The first story in the series presents our Heavenly Father's Plan of Salvation and takes place in the Pre-Earth World. Now, of course, because we all—when we were born—received what is known as The Veil of Forgetfulness, I do not actually remember everything from or about the Pre-Earth World, but I do know about and understand it from much study and worship as a member of The Church of Jesus Christ of Latter-Day Saints, and memories restored to me through the Holy Spirit. So, from this story there is much truth to be learned.

The last story in the series is set in the Post-Mortal World, and presents a depiction of what happens to us after this life. Again, because I have not gone there yet, I cannot say I 'remember' this. But, I have also learned about the Post-Mortal World from much study and worship as a member of The Church of Jesus Christ of Latter-Day Saints.

All of the other stories are based on true events from my life, events that actually occurred when and how they are depicted in these stories. I chose these events because they are among the many occurrences in my life that presented—or revealed that which I already knew without having to be taught—Principles of Eternal Truths.

Also, I chose these events as the settings for my stories because they depict wonderful learning moments from my childhood and adolescent years, lessons that have blessed and benefited me throughout the whole of my life and will forever continue to do so. Also, through these great truths and their consequences in my life, I have been able to share them with many others, whose lives have also been blessed by them.

So, please read and enjoy, then care and share the messages and stories with others!!

Now, there are also a couple of things you can look for:

In each story, the title of the previous story is presented in *italicized* form, the title of the next story is presented in *Capitalized Italicized* form, and the title of the story being read is presented in **emboldened** form.

2

Also, every story has at least one word that is uncommon or 'created.'

So, as you read, search, find, and have fun!

SOMETHING TO BE PROUD OF

Ellie came bursting through the church doors and bounding down the stairs with all the energy of a steam-powered locomotive engine. Well, okay maybe not that much, but she sure was filled with excitement about something! That was why, even though it was an "Eyore" kind of day, overcast with a blanket of grey clouds and gloomy, gloomy, gloo... well, you know what I mean. Anyway, even though it was not a bright, sunshiny day, which was the kind of day Ellie loved the most, she was as happy as a honeybee in a blooming flower garden!

After 'bouncing' off the bottom step of the stairs, Ellie hopped, skipped, and jumped her way to the curb. As she stopped to look both ways, left and, to make certain there were no cars coming. Before she began to cross 7th Avenue, she heard Tricia, her cousin, calling from the top of the stairs, "Ellie, wait for me!"

Now, on most days, Ellie would stop in her tracks, stand almost still, which was quite the accomplishment for her, and wait for Tricia to catch up.

4

'Wait a minute!' you might be asking yourself, 'Why would something that simple, just standing still, be so hard for her?' Well, if you are asking yourself that question that means you do not have the answer for it. So, I will answer that question for you.

You see, while Ellie knew full well that she was always supposed to wait for Tricia and not start to leave without her, that was a little frustrating and quite challenging for her because it seemed, to everyone, that Ellie was always in a hurry to get everywhere, especially home. And, it was also next to impossible for Ellie to keep herself still long enough to wait for anyone or anything. So, since Ellie's class was usually the first one to be dismissed, and Tricia's class was usually the last one to be dismissed, to Ellie, it seemed to take a month of Sundays and two or three Julys before Tricia's class came out of the building.

Now, even though Ellie's response would typically be something like, 'I know, I know,' spoken with all the irritation a generally happy, too cooperative, eight-year-old little girl could muster, which was really not very much, on most days she would still comply, stopping in exactly the spot she was standing in when she heard Tricia's voice. But that day was not like most days.

"Hurry up!" Ellie called to her. "You are such a slow poke!"

Ellie jumped off the curb and began skipping across the street. It was pretty clear that she really was in a hurry to get home, even more of a hurry than usual. So, by the time Tricia caught up with her, she was already on the far side of the street, hopping up onto that curb.

"Can't you walk like normal people?" Tricia complained, when she caught up with Ellie and grabbed her sleeve.

"Nope!" Ellie replied. "Nope! Nope! Nope!"

As they continued down Franklin Street, Tricia was almost running to keep up with Ellie, which was the reverse of how things typically went. That was highly unusual because most of the time, it was Ellie who was just about always running to keep up with everyone. Being as little as she was, and her steps being no longer than you would expect steps to be for someone as little as she was, she always had to hustle to keep up with everyone, even when they were walking at a pace that was slow for them, or so they would say.

"What's with you?" Tricia asked as they shuffled up Franklin Street.

"I do not know," Ellie teased, "What are you?"

"Very funny," Tricia said, trying to sound annoyed, but she could not, because she was not. Like everyone else, Tricia liked the way Ellie could play with words. It always added fun to every conversation! "I mean," she added, "what's wrong with you?"

"Nothing," Ellie said. "Nothing, nothing, nothing."

"Then why are you in such a hurry?" Tricia asked.

"Because," Ellie explained, "I have the greatest thing in the world to tell my daddy and mommy; it is the greatest thing that ever happened to me."

"What is it?" Tricia asked curiously.

As Ellie hopped, skipped, jumped, loped... well, you know what I am saying, as she did everything but walk, she told Tricia all about what happened in class, and what Sister Anne had said to her when she gave her the bag that held the missal and rosary that her daddy and mommy had ordered for her First Holy Communion Ceremony.

"It was not a very good class today," Ellie began. "Pennie gave all the wrong answers to the catechism questions that Sister Anne asked her. When Sister Anne scolded her for not studying more and told her that was nothing to be proud of, Pennie started to cry. I think Sister Anne probably felt kind of bad for not being nice to Pennie, because she took her to the hall to help her calm down. That was when Nestor started picking on Hinkley."

"Why?" Tricia asked with amazement. She knew Nestor, and knew that he was a pretty nice kid, and was usually pretty well behaved, well, at least for a little boy.

7

"'Cause," Ellie replied, "Nestor got in trouble in school, and he was still in a bad mood."

"Oh!" Tricia said, somewhat surprised, then added, "Poor Hinkley."

"Not really," Ellie said. "Hinkley was in a bad mood because he got in trouble at school too. I do not know what he did, but I know that was why Mrs. L'Nels would not let him go to the playground for recess."

"Gee," Tricia replied quizzically, "I wonder what they did."

"I do not know," Ellie restated, "but I do know that was why they were both in pretty bad moods, and that was also why, when Nestor bopped Hinkley on the noggin with a pencil, Hinkley pushed Nestor off his chair. Then, Nestor got up and pushed Hinkley off his chair. So, Hinkley kicked Nestor on the right knee, and Nestor stomped on Hinkley's left foot. That was when the rest of the boys took sides and started cheering for Nestor or Hinkley, until Sister Anne came back in the room and yelled at them to stop."

"Yelled?" Tricia asked a bit disbelievingly. That was not like Sister Anne. Sure, she could sound pretty nasty when she got upset with someone, but Tricia had never heard her yell.

"Yeah, yelled," Ellie replied strongly, "just like Mrs. Tipsey did when her puppy pottied in the parlor and chewed up her best pair of sneakers."

Side Note: Mrs. Tipsey was one of the Stations', that is Ellie's family, down-the-street neighbors, and she was a pretty grumpy lady. She was always upset with someone about something. And when she was not upset with someone, she was upset with her poor little puppy, who seemed to get into trouble for everything, anything, and nothing at all. Now, back where we were before we stepped to the side.

Tricia could not help but laugh at Ellie's comment about Mrs. Tipsey and her poor little puppy. Her family lived just six houses down and across the street from the Tipsey's and she remembered that incident. In fact, there was probably no one in the neighborhood who did not remember it. When Mrs. Tipsey got upset, and it did not take much for that to happen, everybody on both sides of the world knew about it. Well, okay, maybe not everybody on both sides of the world, but at least everyone all across the state of Pennsylvania. Mrs. Tipsey was never quiet about anything.

"Why did Sister Anne yell?" Tricia wanted to know.

"She was really mad," Ellie said. Then, to show Tricia what happened, she shook her pointer finger at Tricia, the way Sister Anne had shaken her pointer finger at Nestor and Hinkley, and continued to explain, "She told them there was no good reason to ever behave badly and they were not behaving goodly in God's house, and that was nothing to be proud of.

Then she made them stand in two different corners for the rest of the class. She even got mad at me."

"You?!" Tricia asked in amazement. "You never get in trouble with Sister Anne!"

"I know," Ellie replied, with a confident tone of innocence.

"So, what did you do?" Tricia asked.

"Nothing," Ellie said matter-of-factly, "nothing, nothing, nothing."

"Okay," Tricia said, and then asked, "What didn't you do?"

"Nothing," Ellie said again just as matter-of-factly, "nothing, nothing, nothing."

"Ellie," Tricia was getting a little frustrated now. "If you did nothing and you didn't do nothing, then why did Sister Anne get mad at you?"

"Because," Ellie explained innocently, "she did not know the right answer to the question she asked me, so I had to tell her what it was."

"She didn't know the answer?" Tricia asked; she knew where this was going. With Ellie, it went there a lot!

"That is right," Ellie replied, "and when I told her what it was, she got mad."

"Again, Ellie?" Tricia asked, "What was the question this time?"

"She asked me what the Trinity was," Ellie answered, again, quite matter-of-factly.

"Soooo, what did you tell her?" Tricia asked, curiously. She could not imagine what Ellie might have said that would have upset Sister Anne.

"Well, first I gave her the answer that was in the catechism, word-for-word," Ellie explained, "but then I told her it was wrong."

"Oh, Ellie," Tricia said with a 'not again' expression and a bit of concern, then asked, "what did she do?!

"Well, first, she slammed her pen down on the desk, then she looked at me over her glasses, like this," Ellie did her best to imitate Sister Anne, by lowering her head and raising her eyes, as she looked at Tricia. Doing her best to imitate Sister Annes' vocal tone, Ellie then repeated to Tricia what Sister Anne had said, which was, "'Ellie Stations, What do you mean?'"

"I told her that God, Jesus, and the Holy Ghost are three different people."

"Whoa, so what did she do after that?" Tricia asked, but not with too much surprise or alarm. Ellie did this a lot and she never really got in trouble for it, not with her daddy, but then Ellie never got in trouble with her daddy, not with her mommy, and not even with Sister Anne, well, maybe a little bit with Sister Anne, but just a little, a very little.

Now, **Side Note:** Sister Anne probably would have put Ellie in trouble, if her daddy had not made it very clear to all their teachers that he would not tolerate the type of discipline that was commonly used in too many of the schools at that time, which, by the way, was a long time ago. He had told all of them, "If there is a problem with one of my children, you let me know and I will take care of it. But you do not touch them!" So, that was why the Station's kids never got hit with a paddle! If there was a problem, and that did not happen often, they were given notes to take home. Now, back to the other side.

"She gave me a note to take home to my daddy and mommy," Ellie replied, in a 'what she always does' tone.

"Oh, that's all?" Tricia was a little confused. "So, is that what you're in a hurry to tell your daddy and mommy?"

"No!" Ellie laughed. "I often take notes home, just about every time I answer a catechism question."

Now, Tricia did know that, and she knew that Ellie never did get in trouble for it. Actually, it seemed to her that what Ellie said the right answers made more sense than what the Catechism said the right answers were. Anyway, at that point, Tricia was beginning to run low on patience and demanded to know, "Then what is it?"

After jumping over a bunch of cracks and two lines on the pavement, so as to not 'break any backs or die at thirty-nine, Ellie began again to tell Tricia about her day in class.

'Wait! Wait!' How does that make any sense? you are probably wondering. Well, just in case you are, and even if you are not, I will remind you. When Ellie was a little girl, which, as I said before, was a pretty big bit of time ago, there was a silly saying that just about all the kids said and did. It went like this: 'Step on a crack, break your mother's back, step on a line, die at thirty-nine.' So, every time they walked anywhere, they avoided cracks and lines in the pavements by walking around them on jumping over them. And Ellie was one of those kids who did that all the time. Now, back to her tale about their day in class.

As I said, Ellie began with, "Well, it was not a very good class today. Father Wags came in twice. The first time, he just talked to Sister Anne in the back of the room, but the second time, she left the room with him.

"That was when Pauly started making fun of me for giving the right answer. When he called me a stupid shrimp, Terry threw a book at him. Of course, that made Pauly mad, so he picked up the book and was going to throw it back at Terry. But Sister Anne came back in just as Pauly was about to throw the book and she grabbed it out of his hand. Then, after questioning everyone to find out what happened, she sent Terry to an empty corner for throwing the book at Pauly, and she sent Pauly to the last corner for making fun of me. She told them what they did was nothing to be proud of."

"Well," Tricia said, "Terry should not have thrown a book at Pauly, but I am glad to know that he stood up for you. Pauly sure was not being nice." After giving Ellie a little 'hand hug,' she asked, "So, what did Sister Anne do then?"

"I know she was really upset about something," Ellie began, "but I do not know what it was. It did not seem to be just what was going on in class, because she was even more disturbed after Father Wags talked with her. Anyway, it was pretty obvious to all of us that something was really bothering her. So, when she went back to her desk, she plopped down on her chair, put her face in her hands and sighed, and sighed, and sighed.

"I thought she was going to cry, but she did not. Instead, she told us to get out our rosaries and then she said, (Ellie lowered her voice and spoke with authority, trying to sound like Sister Anne), "'Children, this has not been a good day; I think we should all pray.' So, we did; we recited all the prayers together, again, and again, and ag..."

"Okay, Ellie," Tricia interrupted, "I get it; you prayed a lot."

"Yep," Ellie replied, "we prayed until it was time to go. But when she said it was time to line up at the door, it was not really time to go. So, we, well I, asked her why we were leaving so early; I asked her if she was tired of us. She looked at me with a sad expression, but also a little hint of a smile and said, (Again, Ellie tried to sound like Sister Anne), 'No, Ellie, I could never be tired of you,' and then she smiled a big smile at me."

"Soooo, is that what you want to tell your daddy and mommy?" Tricia asked, not really believing, but thinking maybe that was the reason for Ellie's excitement.

"No," Ellie replied and continued as if there had never been an interruption, "she told us it was delivery day and the things we ordered had come in, so we were going to the supply closet to get our stuff for our First Holy Communion Ceremony. THAT was when the greatest thing that ever happened to me, happened."

"So, what was it?!" Tricia asked with a little bigger bit of impatience and a lot bigger bit of curiosity. To Ellie, just about everything was the greatest thing that ever happened to her, until the next greatest thing that ever happened, happens. So, it was not possible for Tricia to try to figure it out for herself.

"Well, you know how, because everyone thinks I am so small, even for an eight-year-old, that I always get put in the front of the line?" Ellie began.

"You are small, Ellie," Tricia interjected.

"Well today," Ellie continued, again as if there had been no interruption, pretending to not have heard what Tricia said, "I did not get put in the front of the line. To make it easier for Sister Rose to hand out the things we were getting, Sister Anne lined us up the way our names were on her order list, so I got put behind Lindy, who was behind Sarah, who came after Mikey, who stood next to Lee."

"Ellie," Tricia, knowing how detailed Ellie liked to be, interrupted again, "you don't have to tell me how everyone lined up. Just tell me what happened."

"Okay," Ellie replied compliantly, and then continued. "After we all were in line, Sister Anne took us all the way to the other end of the hall, past the chapel and the big kids' classrooms. That's where the supply closets are.

"When we got there, Sister Anne told us to stand against the wall until it was our turn to get our stuff. While we were standing there, waiting for Sister Rose to come, I noticed that Sarah was searching through all her pockets and her book bag for something. Then, she started to cry. When Sister Anne asked her what was wrong, she said she could not find *the ring* her daddy had given her for her birthday. She had looked everywhere she thought it could have been but could not find it. I knew that it must have meant a lot to her, so I asked Sister Anne if I could help Sarah look for it and she said that would be okay. So, I started looking around and, sure enough, it only took a couple of minutes for me to find it. It was on the floor right by the water fountain. I picked it up and gave it to Sister Anne and she handed it to Sarah. Sarah was so happy! She gave me a great big 'little hug' and said thank you a trazillion times!

"And that is what you are excited to tell your daddy and mommy," Tricia said, with excitement, certain that she had finally figured it out.

"No," Ellie said simply, then continued. "When Sister Rose was there, to help hand out the stuff, and since we were already in the right order, Sister Anne said we could just come up when the kid in front of us was done. So, Lee was first; he just got a missal. So did Mikey, and he was next. Sarah was after him; she got a veil, gloves, her dress, and a missal, and Lindy got a veil, gloves, shoes, socks and a rosary. Then it was my turn.

"Sister Anne reached into the box and pulled out a bag that had a veil, socks, gloves, a rosary, and a missal in it. When she tried to hand it to me, I told her, 'Sister Anne, that is not mine.'"

"Yes, it is," she said back to me.

"No," I told her, "I did not get a veil, socks, or gloves; I only got a missal and a rosary."

"No," Sister Anne said, "the list shows that you get a veil, socks, and gloves too."

Then I told her, "But, when I gave you the paper that my daddy gave to me to give to you, it did not have on it a veil or socks or gloves because I have my own shoes and socks, and I am going to wear my sister's dress, slip, veil, and gloves. All I am supposed to get is a missal and a rosary."

"Are you sure?" she asked me.

"Yup, uh-huh," I told her, "That was all we ordered and that is all I can take, because that is all that my daddy gave me the money for. I cannot take something that we did not pay for. That would not be right.

"She stared at me for a few minutes with a funny look on her face, then she took me out of the line and told me to wait by the classroom that was across the hall from the closet. She said she needed to check with Sister Rose. Sister Rose said she had to go somewhere else to look at something else to find out, so Sister Anne continued to hand out the stuff until she came back.

"While we waited, she gave a missal, veil, and gloves to Pennie. Terry was next; he got a missal and a rosary, and so did Pauly, Hinkley, and Nestor. That was when Sister Rose came back. She had a long, long, really long, longer than a kite's tail list with her, and when she showed it to Sister Anne, she told her that I was right; I only get a missal and a rosary.

"Sister Anne looked at me for a long time, then she did start to cry, and that was when the greatest thing that ever happened to me, happened."

Because Ellie paused for a full split second, Tricia, who just could not wait any longer to know, asked, "What was it? What happened?!"

"Sister Anne looked at me and started to cry," Ellie said in a most lovingly, joyful tone. "Then, she knelt down in front of me, gave me a great big hug, and said, 'Ellie, thank you for being so honest! That is the way God wants you to be, and He loves you for it! And, Ellie that is truly **something to be proud of!**'"

"Wow!" Tricia said with awe, as she stopped in her tracks, took Ellie's hand and turned her around to face her. She was genuinely impressed with and proud of her cousin, "That really is **something to be proud of**," she said to Ellie, "and I am really proud of you and happy that you're my cousin!"

Tricia gave Ellie her second big hug of the day and together, they skipped the rest of the way to Ellie's house where. As they hopped through the back door, which opened to the kitchen, Ellie, who felt like she was already in heaven, said to Tricia, with super excitement, *"Now I Am Home,* and I can tell Daddy and Mommy, Jeanie, Junior, and Maria all about what had happened at catechism! Then, I will go to your house with you and I can even tell your mom and dad and sisters!"

And why not? After all, she definitely did have **something to be proud of!**

ABOUT THE AUTHOR

Eileen DiStasio-Clark is the second oldest of four children. She is the mother of eleven children and grandmother to twenty-three grandchildren, to date. As a member of The Church of Jesus Christ of Latter-Day Saints, she serves in various positions, teaching, leading, and ministering to children, youth, and adults. Currently, she is also a Family History Missionary. Eileen established the Pursuit of Excellence Institute of Family Education, a non-profit organization focused on strengthening the family. Presently she holds an AA, a BA, and an MA in Clinical Psychology and is working on the completion of her Doctoral Degree.

Milton Keynes UK
Ingram Content Group UK Ltd.
UKHW050920231124
451587UK00021B/297

9 798330 556274